MORE
COUNTRY WALKS
— IN THE —
RUGBY AREA

Jim Watson

Commemorative stone to the
Jurrasic Way on Honey Hill

Good working!
Jim Watson

THISWAY
BOOKS

RUGBY • WARWICKSHIRE

THISWAY BOOKS

Thisway Books, 25 Frobisher Road, Rugby, Warwickshire CV22 7HU
Tel/fax: 01788 813609. e-mail: jimartwatson@btinternet.com

PLEASE NOTE

All these walks are on public rights of way. Most are well-established and it's usually obvious where you can walk. There may, however, be occasional short sections where waymarking has disappeared, fences have been moved, or crops have been planted across the path. Don't panic. Use your common sense. This is the rural Midlands. You can't get lost. Can you?

The sketchmaps are schematic and intended only as guides. Ordnance Survey Explorer maps sheets 206 221, 222 and 223 cover all of the walks and are highly recommended.

The walks cross farmland so you will certainly come across farm animals. Assume all of them to be dangerous, even though it's highly unlikely that any of them are – as long as they are

left alone. If animals approach you they are probably only being nosy. However, if you have a dog with you they might see it as a threat and could become aggressive to protect their young. Don't run away. They'll think it's a game and will join in like big, boisterous children.

Keep to the paths but if anything scary blocks your way you are within your rights to find another route round the obstruction.

Serious incidents, paths blocked or in poor condition should be reported to the appropriate county council: Warwickshire Tel: 00845 090 7000, Northamptonshire Tel: 01604 236 236.

The author also welcomes news of any changes or problems.
Good walking!

Contents

Symbols used on the maps

 Walking route   Gate   Stile   Foot bridge   Kissing gate

 Parking   Church with spire   Church with tower   Bridge   Buildings

To save space 'right' and 'left' are abbreviated to 'R' and 'L' and 'right hand side' and left hand side' to 'RHS' and 'LHS'.

Hungerfield Bridge

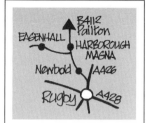

Start & finish Easenhall, off the B4112 Pailton road, four miles north of Rugby.
Parking Rear car park of the Golden Lion by kind permission of the landlord, Jim Austin.
Terrain Field paths and tracks. One gentle climb.
Time Allow two hours.
Facilities The Golden Lion.
Map Explorer sheet 222.

This easy walk explores the countryside around the small village of Easenhall. With red brick farm buildings, a historic country estate and some good views, it's a route for all the family to enjoy.

1 Starting from the Golden Lion car park turn L along the pavement towards the village green. After about 25 yards cross the road and go down an enclosed pathway between two private gardens. Keep straight ahead across two fields and go over the railway footbridge. Head across another field and go over the Oxford Canal bridge. Follow the remnants of an old hedge on your L downhill to Cathiron Lane.

Turn R along the lane for about 400 yards then turn R up a rough lane to the hamlet of Hungerfield. Follow the lane L over the canal bridge. Keep on the lane as it swings R through the yard of Town Thorns Farm to the Easenhall to Brinklow road. Cross – with care! – to a tree-lined drive opposite.

At the top of a gentle rise where the drive swings L, our route keeps straight

Entrance to Manor Farm

on into a rough lane. Go past a small sewage plant and swing R to walk along the edge of a field for about 40 yards. Then turn L through a broad opening and immediately turn R to walk along the side of another field with a small wood on your R. At the end of the field climb a stile and cross the next field to go over the railway footbridge.

2 Continue diagonally across the next two fields and go through an iron farm gate onto a rough track. Turn R towards a wood with the extensive grounds of Newbold Revel on your L.

The grand mansion, now a college for prison officers, was built in 1716 and is famous as the home of Sir Thomas Malory (died 1471) who is generally considered to be the author of *Le Morte D'Arthur*. Ironically, the classic retelling of the Arthurian legends was written while the author was in prison.

When you emerge from the wood turn sharp L and follow the edge of the wood. Cross two wooden footbridges and turn R along the edge of a field.

3 Continue on the obvious path up a gently-rising hillside with good views across the surrounding countryside. Go down the other side of the hill to join a lane at Welkin Farm which brings you back into Easenhall.

The village was built for workers on the Newbold Revel and may be named from its position east of the hall. Walk up the main street past three sets of solid Victorian semis, red-bricked and each with its own gable design.

The Golden Lion dates from 1640 and still has part of the original wattle and daub walls on display in the bar.

A tiny, fairy-tale cottage stands by the village green, one of the prettiest in the area. There's also a huge barn with a vast gateway framing red-brick Manor Farm.

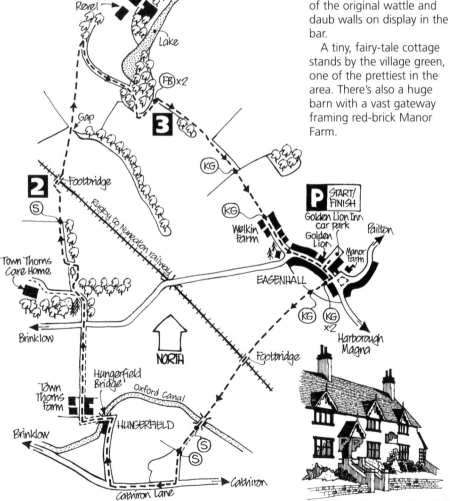

The Golden Lion, Easenhall

5

Garden Cottage, Wappenbury

A wonderful little walk across the peaceful countryside bordered by the busy Fosse Way and the Princethorpe to Weston road. It links three ancient settlements and is full of interest throughout.

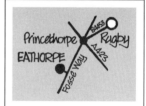

Start & finish Eathorpe, seven miles south west of Rugby.
Parking The Plough car park, Eathorpe (Patrons only).
Terrain Field paths and lanes.
Time Allow two hours
Facilities The Plough at Eathorpe. The Red lion at Hunningham.
Map Explorer sheet 221.

1 Turn R out of The Plough car park onto a narrow road. This soon turns sharp L and goes down a hill into the village. At the tee junction turn R and cross the bridge over the River Leam out of Eathorpe.

Keep on the road for 200 yards or so, then go over a stile in the fence on your R into an open field. Follow the fence on your L and pass a weir in the river. Climb a stile into the next field.

Keep L of a grassy mound in the field and head for the far LH corner ahead. Go through the LH of the two metal gates in the corner. Keeping to the hedge on your R, cross two fields and climb gradually to rough ground near Wappenbury Hall.

The Hall was once the home of Sir William Lyons (1901-85), the founder of Jaguar cars. Go through a metal gate on your R and, following the high hedge around the hall, descend to the Wappenbury to Eathorpe road.

2 Turn L along the road past the hall then, opposite the entrance, turn R down the lane to the

The Mill House, Eathorpe

ancient Church of St John the Baptist at Wappenbury.

Sir William Lyons and Samual Shepheard of Eathorpe are buried here, also Frank Henry Bluemel, the bicycle-pump manufacturer. This area was once a large Iron Age earthwork and Romano-British remains have been found in the fields east of the village.

Join the lane heading away from the church, passing a sign warning 'No Vehicles'. When you come to the gate of a small plantation, climb a stile in the hedge on your L into a field. Descend to a pretty stone footbridge over the Leam and keep straight on across a field. Join an obvious path which keeps to the hedge on your R across three fields to Hunningham.

3 The route continues back up the lane on your L, but first it's well-worth turning R and walking through the small village for a look (and possible refreshment) at the The Red Lion, an attractive hostelry set beside a 14th century stone bridge over the River Leam. Return up the hill through the village and take the lane L to Hunningham Farm. Bear R through the farm buildings to join a bridleway which undulates pleasingly across fields above the river.

4 Watch for a gap in the hedge on your L where you should leave the

The Plough at Eathorpe

bridleway and walk along a narrow field beside the river. Climb a stile in the far RH corner into the next field. Keep to the hedge on your L and climb a double stile into the corner of a field. Cross straight over the short distance to a stile into the quiet road which goes back to Eathorpe.

Turn L along the road and pass the fine-looking Eathorpe Hall and its dinky little gatehouse. The

18th-century red-brick hall was the home of Samuel Shepheard (1816-66), who made his fortune in Egypt. Born at Daventry and brought up at Leamington, he retired to Eathorpe in 1860 and is buried at Wappenbury. His initials and the date 1862 can be seen on several Eathorpe cottages and on the bridge over the Leam.

Keep straight on at a tee junction passing the new village hall. Continue along the single village street where there are some attractive cottages to enjoy. Turn R at the tee junction where the walk started and retrace your steps back to the Plough Inn for suitable postwalk refuelling.

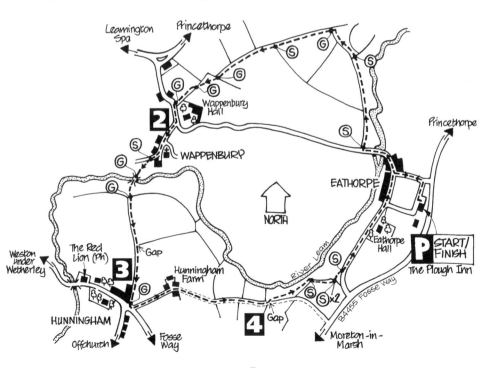

Withybrook

Start & finish Withybrook, seven miles north west of Rugby.
Parking Grass triangle at the junction of Overstone Road and Featherbed Lane.
Terrain Varied: Field paths, canal towpath tracks, farm estate roads and minor roads.
Time Allow two hours.
Facilities The Pheasant Inn at Withybrook.
Map Explorer sheet 222.

A varied walk across open country with some fine views. A good route to discover the pleasures of the sometimes forgotten countryside bordered by the Fosse Way and the M6 and M69 motorways.

1 Begin walking along Featherbed Lane back to the main road and turn R along it. After about 50 yards turn L into a waymarked bridleway and follow the hedge on your R to the bottom of the field. Keep to the the hedge as it swings L and go through a double gate. Follow the hedge on your L and keep on the bridleway across a couple of fields to a triangular-shaped boggy area (The Springs) which you may have to find a way round after rain.

Keep on the bridleway until you approach the rear of Hopsford Springs farm. Go through a gate in a wooden fence and immediately turn L to go down a hill to the Withybrook to Shilton road.

Turn R along the road to pass the front of Hopsford Springs farm. Climb a hill to the couple of houses which make up the hamlet

Hopsford Hall

of Hopsford. Continue round a sharp corner and into a dip in the road.

2 When the road begins to rise again turn L through an open gate onto a narrow, metalled road signed 'Hopsford Hall'.

Pass a fishing lake on your L and after a half mile of level walking arrive at Hopsford Hall. Go through a gate straight ahead and into a green lane. This sweeps L past Chestnut trees then R across rough ground to a high railway embankment. Go through the two tunnels beneath the railway and the Oxford Canal, each a considerable feat of

8

engineering.

When you emerge, turn immediately L to climb the canal bank and turn R along the towpath. Keep walking for about 500 yards until you approach a metal bridge high above the canal and railway. At a brick-built restriction in the width of the canal, turn R through a broken-down metal gate onto rough ground and climb a steep hill to the lane at the top.

3 Pause to take in the extensive view across the M6 motorway to the factory buildings at Ansty and the tower blocks of Coventry beyond. The view to the north is more countrified with the golf course at Shilton prominent and farmland – some you have just crossed – stretching into the distance.

Cross the bridge and pass a house on your R, ignoring the sign which states 'Private Road, no bridleway'. This is part of the Centenary Way and walkers are welcome.

When the lane swings R to Mobbs Wood Farm, turn L onto a path which goes alongside a wooden fence across the front of the farmhouse. Go over a stile into a long, narrow meadow. Head diagonally up the slope of the field to the far corner of the wood on your R.

4 The Centenary Way continues straight ahead between two patches of woodland, but our route turns L. Go over a stile into an enclosed pathway between a high hedge and a wooden fence.

Proceed downhill into a green lane which continues to descend gently to the Shilton to Withybrook minor road. Keep straight on along the road which joins the Pailton road back into Withybrook village.

5 There's sustenance at The Pheasant Inn but first you may wish to take the lane straight ahead for a look at the pretty Church of All Saints, picturesquely set on a hillock with a brook twinkling by.

Return to the main road and turn R along the village main street. At the first junction out of the lower part of the village turn R into a narrow road which climbs past a garden centre and back to Featherbed Lane at the top of the hill.

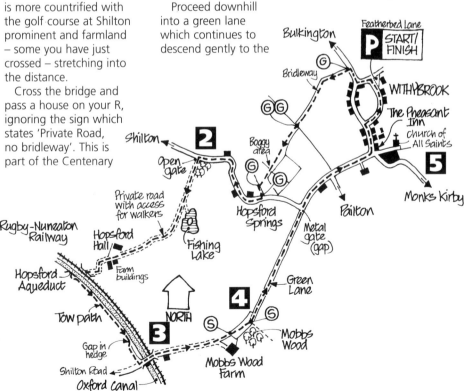

9

4. Wolston, Bretford & Brandon   3.5 miles/5.6 km

Main Street, Wolston

Start & finish Wolston, six miles west of Rugby.
Parking Village hall car park or with discretion on the main street.
Terrain Field paths, bridleways and roadsides. Expect mud after rain.
Time Allow two hours.
Facilities Pubs: The Rose and Crown and The Red Lion at Wolston, The Royal Oak at Brandon and The Queen's Head at Bretford. General shops in Wolston.
Map Explorer sheet 222.

A short but satisfying stroll which links the two large villages of Wolston and Brandon plus the historic hamlet of Bretford. There's a variety of countryside and good views from high ground above Bretford.

1 Begin at the village green and go down an alleyway next to 'The Old Post Office' to a modern housing estate. Keep walking along Larchfields and Meadow Road. At the end of the estate turn L along Priory Lane. Follow the lane round a sharp RH bend passing The Old Priory on your L. Go under a railway bridge and over a cattle grid onto a bridleway near Marston Hall Farm.

2 Continue to Marston Mill farmhouse and pass farm buildings onto a way-marked dirt track which takes you through meadows on the banks of the Avon. Climb slightly to a tree-lined path above the river to reach the Bretford to Wolston road beside a bungalow.

Turn L along the road and with care – it's a busy road – walk the short distance to the junction with the Rugby to Bretford A428 road. Turn L along a roadside footpath and cross the ancient, five-arched roadbridge over the Avon, which dates back to 1279,

House at Bretford

into Bretford. Set on the Fosse Way, the hamlet was a planned 'new' town during the Middle Ages.

Where the road turns R out of Bretford turn L onto the A428,

10

signposted 'Coventry', then immediately cross the road to a lane signposted 'Bretford Village Hall'. Pass the hall and climb on a sunken track to a narrow bridleway. The route is enclosed by fences and very popular with horse riders so is easy to follow, but can also be rough and muddy after rain.

3 Continue to a junction of bridleways, turn L for about 100 yards then turn L again onto another waymarked bridleway. Follow the obvious track to join the Rugby to Brandon road at a sharp junction on the north eastern side of the village.

Walk 200 yards or so – with care along the busy road – and enter the 'No entry' road ahead. Immediatey turn R along an elevated footpath in front of a row of houses to avoid walking along a narrow and busy road bottleneck to the village green.

4 Pass some pretty thatched cottages then turn L to follow the one way system road through the village. Keep on the road as it turns sharp L passing 'The Brandon Hall' hotel to join the road back to Wolston.

Go under the railway bridge and cross the 18th-century, sandstone bridge

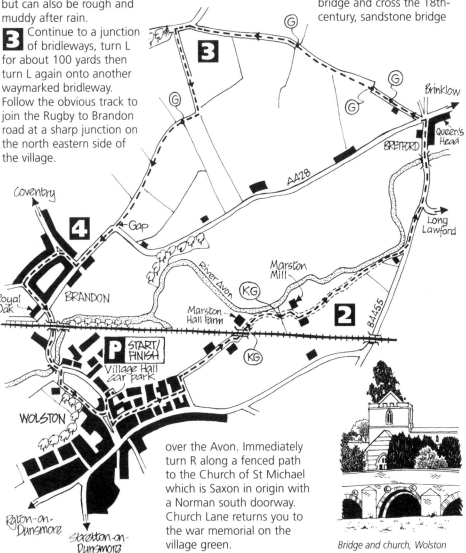

over the Avon. Immediately turn R along a fenced path to the Church of St Michael which is Saxon in origin with a Norman south doorway. Church Lane returns you to the war memorial on the village green.

Bridge and church, Wolston

The Friendly Inn, Frankton

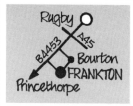

Start & finish Frankton, off the B4453, six miles south east of Rugby.
Parking Car park of the Friendly Inn, Frankton (patrons only).
Terrain Field paths and minor roads. Some hills.
Time Allow two and a half hours.
Facilities The Friendly Inn at Frankton.
Map Explorer sheet 222.

This route across remarkably peaceful countryside links three attractive villages. There's plenty of interest and some terrific views. A lovely little walk.

1 Begin walking down Frankton's attractive main street to the Church of St Nicholas which has a 13th century tower. The next door Manor House was built in 1662. Turn L opposite the church and go through double gates into a field. Keep to wood on your R and climb a hill heading for the far corner of the field. Climb a double stile and head straight across the next field. The view ahead is wide and spectacular with Draycote Water and Rugby to the left and Southam and beyond to the right.

Head for the embankment of the disused Rugby to Leamington railway line, descending steadily to find

a stile in a clump of trees. Cross a narrow meadow to the Bourton to Birdingbury minor road and go through the high-arched bridge beside the River Leam.

Immediately under the bridge turn L up a tarmac drive. After about 150 yards climb a stile on your

Glebe Farm

R into a field and head diagonally for the middle of the fence at the far end. Cross a drive, then a stile and a footbridge and enter a long (almost three quarters of a mile long!) and narrow field. Keep walking parallel with the railway embankment.

2 Eventually, you reach a gate in the far RH corner of the field in sight of Manor Farm on the edge of Draycote village. Cross the next two fields to a stile and turn R along the narrow road past the farm.

Continue on the twisting road for a look at the peaceful village of Draycote. The road ends at Glebe Farm which dates back to the 16th century.

Retrace your steps back

through the village. At a sharp bend just before Manor Farm climb a stile on your R into a field. Go up the slope heading for the far corner of the garden of a private house. Continue to climb while bearing slightly R and go though an arch in the railway embankment.

3 Climb straight up the hill on the other side of the embankment to the appropriately-named Hill Farm. Follow the path around the farmhouse garden then turn sharp L between farm buildings.

Keep to the hedge on your L and go downhill

to find a footbridge to the R of Bog Spinney. Climb out of the dip and follow the hedge on your L as it curves L to join the road into Bourton. A rather mysterious green road parallels the modern version into the village.

Bourton on Dunsmore, which was mentioned, with Draycote, in the Domesday book of 1086, is now an eclectic mix of the ancient and modern and well worth walking through especially when bright with summer flowers. The 'Round House', part of the village hall, was probably once

a toll house and also spent time as Bourton Hall Laundry.

4 The splendid Hall itself dates back to 1791 and has a chequered history including dereliction before its current owners, Ingersoll Engineers, restored it to its present grandeur in 1979.

The early 13th century Church of St Peter stands sombrely at the southern end of the village on the edge of Dunsmore Heath.

Return through the village and turn L at the village hall into the road back to Frankton. Refreshments – and a friendly welcome – are available at the Friendly Inn

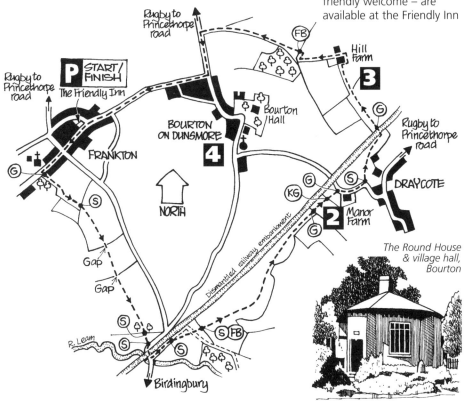

The Round House & village hall, Bourton

13

6. The Lawford Round — 4 miles/6.4 km

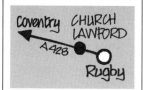

Start & finish Church Lawford, off the A428, three miles west of Rugby.
Parking With consideration on the village streets or in The Old Smithy car park (patrons only).
Terrain Field paths and village streets. Some gentle climbs. Possibility of muddy fields after rain.
Time Allow two hours.
Facilities Pubs at Church Lawford and Long Lawford.
Map Explorer sheet 222.

St Peter's Church tower & the Manor House, Church Lawford

Linking the three Lawford villages, this route crosses prime countryside which narrowly escaped extermination when plans for Europe's largest airport were shelved. Enjoy the walk – and give thanks.

1 Begin walking along Church Road to St Peter's Church which dates back to 1210 but was rebuilt in 1872. Go R through the churchyard and descend a field to a double stile in a thick hedge.

There now follows a gentle meander across four fields with wonderful views across the River Avon. The main road between Rugby and Coventry runs parallel with the route but the sound of traffic is well-muffled by a railway embankment.

As the route begins to rise and turn away from the river cross a double stile on your L and climb a stile into the next field, bearing left to another stile in the hedge on the skyline. Long Lawford village is now seen seen ahead.

2 Go through a kissing gate and turn L along the main street. Pass St John's Church, which is

Footbridge over the Avon

now closed, and take the narrow enclosed bridleway on the LHS of the road. The lane ahead is private and goes to Holbrook Grange, a mansion built by the Caldecott family to replace Little Lawford Hall which stood north of the Avon and was demolished about 1790.

The bridleway gently undulates through farmland to Little Lawford Mill. The road which turns left through the converted mill buildings is private. The right of way is straight ahead, over a stile and into a field. The present Little Lawford Hall, which was adapted about 1800 from stables of 1604, is across the field on your L.

14

Head for the top LH corner of the field and climb a gate onto a road tee junction. Turn left along the road for about 50 yards to another tee junction and climb a stile in the hedge on your R.

3 Cross a large field, first heading for the RHS of one of two trees at the centre, then bear L to climb a stile in a high hedge. Bear R between two ponds, then swing L, climbing slightly, and go over a double stile into a narrow field.

Follow the fence of your L for a short distance, then turn R to cross a field to the corner of a copse of trees around another pond. Keep to the fence on your

R and cross the lane which goes to Fennis Fields Farm.

Climb the stile ahead to join a permissive footpath avoiding the farmhouse. Keep to the hedge on your L and gently climb to the second gate on your L (currently painted white).

4 Go through the gate and climb diagonally across the next field to a gap in the hedge. Bear L across the next field and over the brow of the hill from where there are magnificent views across the countryside to Rugby.

Cross the Little Lawford minor road and, following the way-markers, descend across two fields with

a view of the hamlet of King's Newnham ahead. Keep L of some farm buildings and climb a stile into the next field. Cross diagonally to descend a short, steep hill and cross the River Avon on a footbridge.

5 Keep straight ahead across two fields and enter an enclosed green lane. When you reach a stile don't climb it; instead turn R to follow another green lane which takes you to Smithy Lane and back into Long Lawford.

Bear L up Main Street to the village green and the hospitality of The Old Smithy.

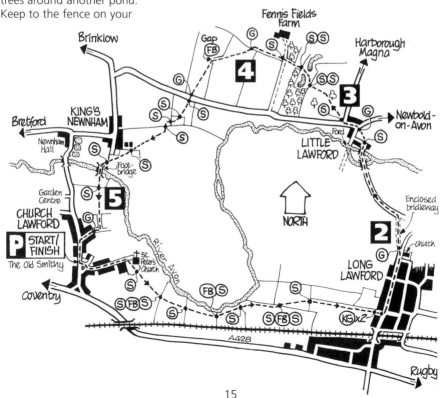

15

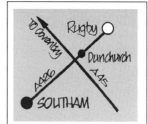

The Black Dog Inn and shops, Southam

Southam is well-worth exploring and this walk is also full of interest. With a deserted mansion, an atmospheric Holy Well, woodland, hills, open fields and good views there's something for everyone.

Start & finish Southam, 10 miles south west of Rugby.
Parking Free car park off Southam main street.
Terrain Field paths and bridleways. Some hills. This route is particularly muddy after rain. Wait for a dry spell for maximum enjoyment
Time Allow two hours.
Facilities Shops, pubs and restaurants in Southam.
Map Explorer sheet 222.

1 Leave the car park, turn L into the Main Street and cross the road to St James' Church. The magnificent 14th century building is best seen from the south side. The 15th century broach spire soars to 126ft (38m).

Leave the churchyard and turn L down Park Lane. At the bottom of the hill turn L down Wattons Lane. When you reach a small industrial area swing R along a narrowing road lined by trees.

The lane opens into a field with the River Stowe to your L. A hard-surfaced path brings you to the Holy Well, sensitively restored in 2006. The spring water is very cold and was once considered to be a remedy for eye infections.

2 Continue on the obvious path to Stoney Thorpe Hall.

The once fine house, currently unoccupied, stands sadly in extensive grounds surrounded by magnificent trees. The 17th century hall was home to Chamberlayne family until 1997. Water provided power for the hall until the 1920s and parts of the original walls can be seen from the footbridge over a weir in the River Itchen.

Cross the footbridge and keep to the bank of the

The Holy Well, Southam

pool on your L. Go over a bridge between the pools and swing R to a metal kissing gate ahead. A footpath continues L up the hill to a superb polo club built by the current owner of the hall at the end of the 1990s.

Our route turns R here to follow the hedge on your R. Climb three stiles and go through a small wood. Cross the Welsh Road – once a drovers route from Wales to London – and enter another wood on a steep, rough and possibly muddy path. After a short climb emerge into an open, hilltop field. Head to a gap in the hedge ahead.

3 Cross the next field heading for the RHS of a agricultural vehicle dump. Continue downhill on a hard surfaced track to the Long Itchington to Harbury Road. Turn R along it through the hamlet of Bascote.

There's a choice of routes

a footbridge over the River Itchen then diagonally cross the next field to a curve in the riverbank.

4 Follow the river to the next hedge then turn L to follow a line of trees on your R. At the top RH corner of the field cross a footbridge and a stile

and keep straight on to a gap in the fence near a school playing field. Head uphill to a housing estate on the edge of Southam. Pass between two blocks of houses and turn R along a long road through the estate. Turn L at the tee junction to pass a primary school and reach the main road through Southam.

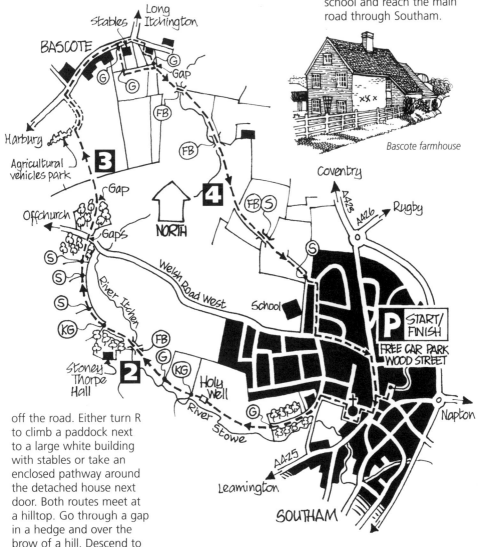

Bascote farmhouse

off the road. Either turn R to climb a paddock next to a large white building with stables or take an enclosed pathway around the detached house next door. Both routes meet at a hilltop. Go through a gap in a hedge and over the brow of a hill. Descend to

17

Church Farm, Weston

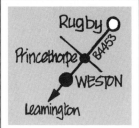

Start & finish Weston under Wetherley, nine miles west of Rugby.
Parking Village Hall car park, Sabin Drive, Weston under Wetherley.
Terrain Field paths and village roads. Expect mud.
Time Allow two and a half hours.
Facilities The King's Head at Cubbington.
Map Explorer sheet 221.

A short, simple, but surprisingly satisfying walk. Straightforward and peaceful on well-used paths with generally good waymarking. Quiet, open countryside with extensive views. An excellent morning or evening walk with the dog (under control).

1 Begin walking along Sabin Drive and turn L at the end along the road through the village of Weston. Just before the road swings right past the church turn L into a green lane opposite Church Farm. Where the lane opens out into a field continue along the top of the field, then before you reach a metal gate ahead, turn R to go downhill and follow the hedge on your L.

Climb a stile on the RHS of a red-brick farm building then turn L through an open gateway. Immediately turn R to follow the hedge on your R. Keep to the hedge, crossing two farm tracks and a long field.

2 Through a gap in the hedge turn L to follow the hedge on your R. Half way along the field side, and beside an old waymarking post, the route abruptly changes direction and turns 135 degrees to cross the open field on your R. The path does continue straight ahead for the short distance to a

King's Head, Cubbington

footbridge over the River Leam. It's worth a look but you will have to retrace your steps back to where the route begins to cross the open field.

Head for a a gap in the high hedge ahead where a waymarking arrow directs you through the gap onto an obvious path which climbs gradually following the hedge and a line of oak trees on your R. As you climb towards South Cubbington Wood an extensive view across lush countryside towards Northampton and Banbury is revealed.

3 Follow the path around the border of the wood and join

Mill Lane, a green lane which soon becomes a hard surfaced road into a modern housing estate on the edge of Cubbington.

Keep walking straight ahead down New Street through the estate to a cross roads where there are striking buildings to admire. There's the Old Manor House with half -timbered walls on one corner, and facing it, The Manor, which looks younger - but not a lot. Opposite, the Parish Church of St Mary stands proudly on a hilltop.

The route turns R here up Church Hill to pass (or pause for a while!) the King's Head. At the top of the hill, where the road sweeps L into Austen Court, keep straight on into an enclosed pathway alongside a children's play area. At the top end of the play area ignore the path going straight ahead (which woud take you to the Rugby Road) and turn R to follow the fence on your R downhill.

4 At the bottom of the hill swing L to

House at Weston

follow the hedge on your R as it climbs steadily away from the village towards the wood ahead. At the top of the hill follow the path L around the edge of the wood. At the top L corner of the field find a path going into the wood.

South Cubbington Wood is pleasant mixed woodland with an odvious path to follow through it. Emerge at the top end of a field sloping down to Weston Hall, a mainly red-brick farm with some large, modern-looking barns. Keep walking downhill

and negotiate an ingenous concrete and metal footbridge which has a bar at each end to hurdle.

5 Turn L along the track to the hall for a short distance then turn R across the bottom of a field with an attractive clump of trees on your L, Keep straight on following the hedge on your L.

As you draw level with the tower of Weston church on your L skyline look out for another concrete footbridge and metal bar contraption in the dense hedge on your L. Cross a narrow field to a stile and climb the next field to join the Princethorpe to Cubbington road at Weston church. Turn R to walk through the village back to the car park at Sabin Drive.

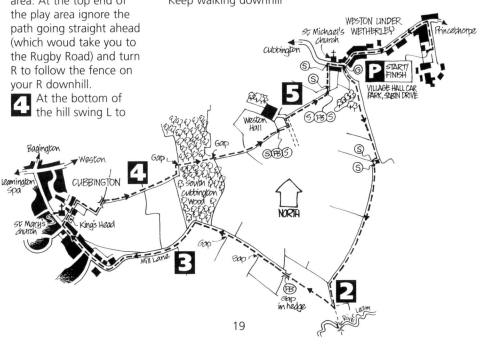

19

Home Farm, Upper Shuckburgh

The Grand Union canal, a peaceful, off-the-beaten-track village, a splendid country park and glorious south Warwickshire countryside make this a summer walk to savour.

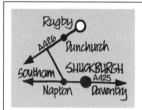

Start & Finish Lower Shuckburgh, eight miles south of Rugby.
Parking Layby at a canal bridge in Lower Shuckburgh or with consideration on the minor road outside the church.
Terrain Field paths, tracks and village streets. Some gentle climbing.
Time Allow two and a half hours.
Facilities The Old Olive Bush pub at Flecknoe.
Map Explorer sheet 222.

1 Cross over the canal bridge to a waymark post on your R. Here you have the choice of the canal towpath or a field path. The towpath is easier walking but you will have to climb a fence to leave it further along.

Keep walking to the first canal bridge you come to (No. 103). Cross it to join a bridleway going diagonally L across an open field. Keep on the bridleway as it climbs gently over two more fields, then turn sharp R to follow a hedge on your R. As the path steepens head for the buildings that can be seen on the skyline.

Go through a field gate by the Old Vicarage to join a lane which takes you into the village.

2 Flecknoe was named in the Domesday Book as 'Flachenho', which possible means 'Flacca's Hill'. It was once part of the parish of Wolfhamcote

The Old Olive Bush, Flecknoe

with Nethercote and Sawbridge but all but Flecknoe were depopulated to make grazing for sheep. During the 19th century the men of Flecknoe were among the first to join Joseph Arch's Agricultural Labourers Union.

The modern village attractively straddles Bush Hill and overlooks the Grand Union Canal and the plain stretching back to Rugby.

Join the road through the village near the village hall, a former school. Head downhill on the road as it sweeps R past an impressive new housing

20

development. Further on there's the Old Olive Bush, a good place to take refreshment. But go easy, across the road sit the old village stocks and they were restored to working order in 1987.

3 Continue walking on the road and turn R at three corners to make a circuit of the village. As you come down the hill towards the village hall turn sharp L up a lane climbing past a farm house.

Follow the lane as it swings L at some farm buildings. When you reach some large barns turn R to follow the hedge on your R, ignoring the more obvious track going L.

Descend gradually to a stile in the corner of the field, then cross four fields on a more or less straight route to the Staverton to Napton road.

Cross with care, then walk L along the roadside for a short distance and turn R into a narrow drive which runs across the eastern boundary of Shuckburgh Hall deer park.

At the lodge turn R into the deer park. The land on your R and the just-glimpsed Shuckburgh Hall – home of the Shuckburgh family since the 11th century – are strictly private so please observe the signs in the park.

4 Walk past the handsome, red-brick Home Farm with its pyramid-roofed dovecot. Where the main track veers R towards the hall keep straight ahead on a rising grassy path. The Church of St John the Baptist in the Wilderness is a fine sight in an elevated position on the edge of the wood to your R.

Keep straight on through the deer park, and at the excellent Millennium brazier begin to descend the fields to Lower Shuckburgh.

Aim for the LH corner of a red-roofed pair of cottages and go through a field gate into another field. Turn L and cross diagonally to a stile in the far R corner.

Cross the Napton to Staverton road (with care!) and, after pausing for a look at the flamboyant Church of St John Baptist, follow the lane back to your car.

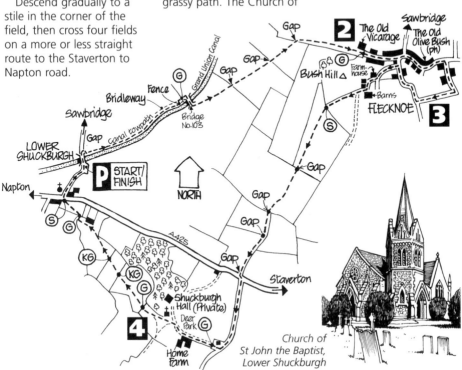

Church of
St John the Baptist,
Lower Shuckburgh

21

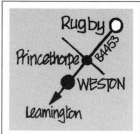

The Old Bakehouse and church at Hunningham

Start & finish Weston under Wetherley, nine miles west of Rugby.
Parking Village Hall car park, Sabin Drive, Weston under Wetherley.
Terrain Field paths and quiet roadsides. Expect mud after rain.
Time Allow two and a half hours.
Facilities The Red Lion at Hunningham.
Map Explorer sheet 221.

An easy-going circuit of three interesting villages, linked by some prime Warwickshire countryside. A restful walk for a minimum of effort.

1 Begin walking north along Sabin Lane and cross the main road. Turn R along the pavement and walk through the village. Weston is a long, strung-out village with a mixture of modern houses and pretty cottages.

At the bottom end of the village, where the road turns sharp L to the Bull Inn, turn R along the road signed 'Hunningham and Long Itchington'. After about 50 yards, climb a stile in the high hedge on your L into a field.

Keep to the hedge on your L and climb another stile. Cross a narrow field using a footbridge over a brook and climb a stile beside a magnificent oak tree into a large field. Keep straight on, climb another stile and go round the perimeter of the next field to the far R corner.

Climb a stile and go over a low hill in the next field to reach a large pond. Turn sharp L, and with the pond on your R, walk along the bank. Turn R over a

St John's Church, Wappenbury

footbridge and, on rising ground, climb a stile into another large field.

2 Keeping L of farm buildings, cross straight across the field and go through a gap in a hedge into a minor road. Turn R down the road to St John's Church. The red stone building has a 15th century tower and is the resting place for a trio of local 'men of distinction'.

Hidden away down the lane beside St John's is St Anne's RC Church which is built onto a cottage where masses were held in secret when the Catholic Morgans were Lords of the Manor.

After visiting the church

go down the lane which is prominently signed 'No Vehicles'.

Beyond the last building, pass through a gate on your L into a field and go down a hill to cross a stone footbridge over the river Leam. Continue straight on across a field and through a gate. Keep on the obvious path along the hedge on your R to Hunningham.

Cross the road in the village and go down the road ahead, passing some semis on your L. Just beyond some farm buildings turn R down a narrow road signed 'Hunningham Church'.

kissing gate and follow the fence L around the churchyard. Go down to the riverside and climb a stile into a green lane on your R which follows the river to an open field. Cross to the Red Lion Inn ahead.

Turn L along the Bubbenhall to Hunningham road and cross the narrow stone bridge over the Leam. The original was medieval but rebuilt in 1651 at a cost of £20.

4 Where the road swings R climb a stile on your L beside a Severn

Trent building and cross a field to the far R corner.

Climb a stile and follow a hedge – first on the LHS and then on the RHS – heading straight for Weston church tower. When you reach an open field cross diagonally to an enclosed lane which emerges back into Weston near the soft sandstone St Michael's Church, parts of which date back to the 13th century.

Turn R and walk through the village back to Sabin Drive.

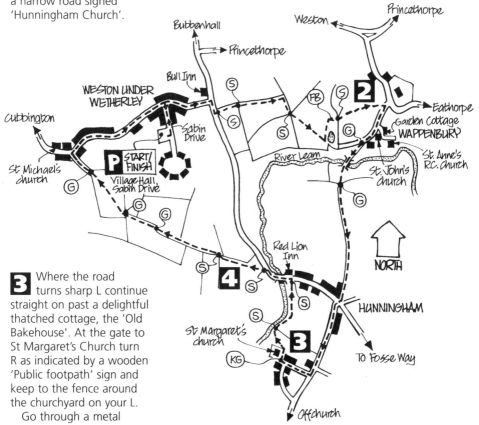

3 Where the road turns sharp L continue straight on past a delightful thatched cottage, the 'Old Bakehouse'. At the gate to St Margaret's Church turn R as indicated by a wooden 'Public footpath' sign and keep to the fence around the churchyard on your L.

Go through a metal

Priors Hardwick

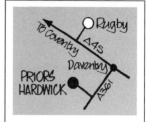

A breezy circuit of prime Northamptonshire farmland which links two picturesque villages and a twisting stretch of the Oxford canal.

Start & finish Priors Hardwick 12 miles south of Rugby.
Parking Roadside at village church or in large car park at The Butcher's Arms (patrons only).
Terrain Mainly field paths across crop fields. Some hills.
Time Allow two and a half hours.
Facilities The Butcher's Arms bar and restaurant, Priors Hardwick.
Map Explorer sheet 206.

1 Begin walking south west along the village road away from St Mary's Church. Turn L at the junction with the Wormleighton to Priors Marston road. Follow the twisting road for a short distance to Old Hill Farm on your L and go through a metal kissing gate opposite into a field. Head up the steep slope bearing R as you climb towards Hill House and the top RH corner of the field. It's worth pausing here to admire the view across the village and the Northamptonshire countryside.

Continue walking along the edge of a wooded escarpment. Go through a kissing gate then descend diagonally across the slope of the hill, keeping topside of a chestnut tree, to go over a stile into the next field. Descend to a waymarked kissing gate and cross a minor road. Go through a gate into a large crop field. Cross the centre of the field heading for distant Stoneton Manor. The aspect is now open with good views. Join the road to the Manor and go through a gate alongside part of a moat which surrounds the building.

Cross the large and

Ancient tower and arch, Wormleighton

rolling crop field in front of you, heading for the distant clump of trees on the skyline. The trees surround Newfield Pool, a pleasant fishing lake hidden away in a fold of the hills, which has some impressive bullrushes and a noisy population of ducks.

2 Head up the hill from the pool and, as indicated by marker poles, cross three flat crop fields to enter the hamlet of Wormleighton. If this is your first visit, prepare to be pleasantly surprised. The small settlement of a large mullion-windowed manor house, a seventeenth

24

century stone tower, Northamptonshire stone cottages with traditional gardens, fine houses, magnificent trees, a thatched terrace, and an ancient church is a delight to explore.

Turn L under the arch of the tower and take a

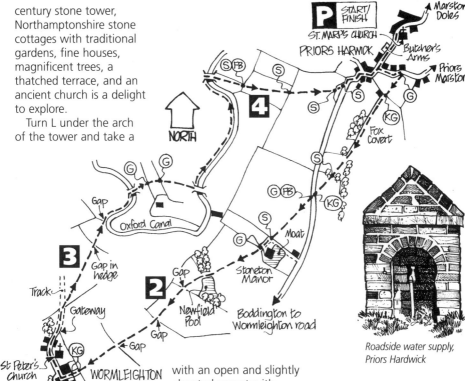

Roadside water supply, Priors Hardwick

wander to the village hall on the main road.

The original Wormleighton village became deserted at the end of the 15th century. The present estate village dates from Victorian times and is owned by the Spencer family. St Peter's Church dates back to the twelfth century but has been much altered and restored since.

Our route continues down the lane to the L of the church. After a short wooded section the lane enters a large crop field

with an open and slightly elevated aspect with terrific views back to Priors Hardwick and beyond.

3 Follow the track around the centre of the field then, just after you pass a hedge on your R, turn R to diagonally cross a large crop field as indicated by a waymark sign. As you descend head for a canal bridge on the other side of the field. When you reach the Oxford Canal follow it round to a bridge (No.127).

Cross the bridge and, as waymarked, cross three fields to another canal bridge (No.126). Climb over a wooden fence on the LH side of the bridge and go onto the towpath. Turn L and walk along

the canalside to the next bridge (No.125). Leave the towpath and cross the canal bridge. Cross a field and go over a stile and a footbridge in the top LH corner.

4 Bear L in the next field and cross to a small gate next to a big metal gate on the other side. Negotiate some large manure heaps in the next field and climb a grassy slope heading for the houses on the skyline. Go through a gate to cross a small field of rough grass to a stile into the road. Turn L for a pleasant meander through Priors Hardwick back to the village centre.

25

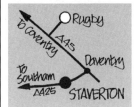

The Village Green, Staverton

A fine walk across farmland straddling the Northamptonshire and Warwickshire border which links the attractive villages of Staverton & Flecknoe. Some terrific views and a pub in each village. Enjoy.

Start & finish Staverton, nine miles south of Rugby.
Parking Around the village green - with consideration please.
Terrain Field paths and bridleways. Some hills. Expect mud.
Time Allow three hours.
Facilities Pubs at Staverton and Flecknoe.
Map Explorer sheet 222.

1 Take the road to the R of the two houses which edge the village green (pictured above). At the junction with the road to the school keep straight on along Braunston Lane.

The view now opens up ahead with the Hillmorton water tower and our old 'friend' the Rugby cement works prominent. The lane dips into rolling Northamptonshire farmland and may be quite rough at the bottom of the hill. However, the inconvenience doesn't last long and on rising ground you're soon back onto a hard surface.

As you climb the hill the spire of Braunston church appears ahead and there's a new view to enjoy. But before you reach the brow of the hill the route turns L

to head towards Flecknoe. The turn off is behind a large mound of farmyard manure, an unattractive but unmissable landmark and all part of the rich pattern of country life. Just watch where you're putting your feet.

Keep to the hedge on your R on the obvious path. It soon descends to cross Miry Bridge, a solid

Fishing Lodge, Flecknoe

wooden structure over the infant River Leam which marks the border between Northamptonshire and Warwickshire.

2 Climb straight up the slope of the field on the other side of the bridge and go through a gate in the hedge ahead. Keep to the hedge on your R and go through a gap into the next field which still bears the surface of ancient ridge and furrow cultivation.

Head for a wooden building which can be seen in the top RH corner of the field but, before you reach the end of the field, bear R to a waymarker which guides you onto a track. Turn L to cross a bridge over a fishing lake, imaginatively created

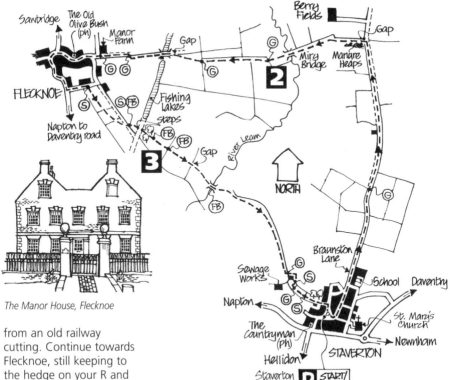

![The Manor House, Flecknoe illustration]

The Manor House, Flecknoe

from an old railway cutting. Continue towards Flecknoe, still keeping to the hedge on your R and join an enclosed, hard-surfaced bridleway to Manor Farm. Go through the farm gate onto a village road, taking care to do as the signs ask, and close the gate behind you. Take the road through the village passing The handsome, twin-gabled Manor House and The Old Olive Bush pub. Bear L up the hill past the village hall and St Marks Church.

Keep on the road, turning L at the next junction. Opposite a row of pink-painted houses turn R off the road and climb a waymarked stile into a field.

Head downhill then, with a railway bridge in sight at the bottom of the hill, bear L to a stile in the hedge. Cross a small paddock to a stile and steps up the disused railway embankment. On the top of the embankment bear slightly R to find steps down the other side. Pass through a short wooded area and keep straight on to find a plank FB over a stream.

3 Cross the next field to another FB in a gap in the hedge ahead into another field. This descends to a concrete FB over the River Leam and back into Northamptonshire.

Head up the hill ahead following the stream on your L up the edge of the field to some stable buildings. Follow the signs around the buildings and through a small yard into a steeply-banked field.

Follow the wire fence on your R up a cutting, climbing to a stile into an enclosed pathway with a babbling brook on your R. Emerge on the LHS of a pebbled area in front of an impressive Northampton stone house, Wellbrook Lodge. Keep to the hedge on your L up Well Lane to join Manor Road. Turn R along it back to Staverton village green.

27

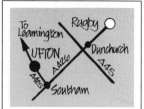

St Michael's Church, Ufton

An easy walk beginning and ending at Ufton Fields Nature Reserve. There's some good views and the attractive villages of Ufton and Harbury to explore.

Start & finish Ufton Fields Nature Reserve, 12 miles south west of Rugby.
Parking Free car park at the reserve.
Terrain Quiet minor roads, bridleways and fields paths.
Time Allow three hours.
Facilities Pubs and shops in Ufton and Harbury.
Map Explorer sheet 221.

1 A circuit of the 100 acre Ufton Fields Nature Reserve can be made at the beginning or end of the cross-country walk. The SSSI, established in 1972 from quarries where lower lias limestone was quarried from 1952 to 1954, now consists of pools, grassed-over ridges and woodland. It is noted for orchids, butterflies and numerous species of birds.

Leave the nature reserve car park and turn L up a minor road towards Harbury. Where the road swings L at Flax Hill, turn R through an open gateway to follow the hedge on your L along the edge of a field. Keep to the hedge and go over another stile. When the hedge turns L, keep straight on across a paddock to another stile.

There are various paddocks for horses around Bull Ring Farm and very clear signs direct you through them onto the farm road. Turn L along the road and climb a hill into Harbury.

2 The village is large and strung out but a circuit of the attractive central section gives a flavour of its attractions. Turn L along Hall Lane and

Gateway into Ufton Fields Nature Reserve

go round the block, passing the Crown Inn in Crown Street to All Saint's Church, notable for the 19th century red-brick top to its tower which sits on a 13th century stone base and a churchyard aglow with daffadils and primroses in springtime.

Go down Church Street and turn L at The Dog Inn along Ivy Lane. Turn R opposite the village hall and recreation field and turn R down Chapel Street, passing The Gamecock (there's no shortage of hostelries in Harbury!) before turning R again up High Street. Follow the one way road system L past The Dog Inn to return down Bull Ring Farm Road to the farm.

At the farm buildings keep to the fence on

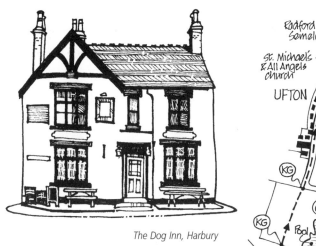

The Dog Inn, Harbury

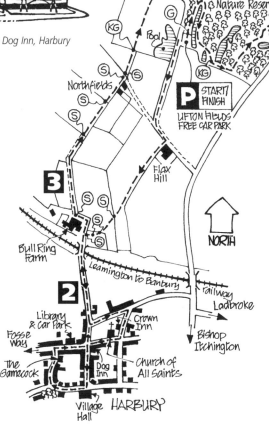

your R and go round the farmyard on an enclosed pathway.

3 Enter a bridleway signed 'Centenary Way', from where there's a terrific view across open countryside to Leamington and Warwick. Keep walking straight across a couple of fields to a quiet minor road into Ufton.

Cross the busy Southam to Leamington road for a look at the mainly 13th century St Michael's Church. Near the gateway there's a 14th century preaching cross with a worn, carved head.

Go down nearby White Hart Lane. It predictably takes you to the White Hart Inn which must have one of the most amazing views across open countryside in the county. A good place to sit outside and take some refreshment.

4 Return along White Hart Lane and re-cross the main road. Turn L past a car salesroom and

just before the far edge of the village turn R into an enclosed pathway at Rectory Lodge. Keep to the hedge on your R on the obvious path which takes

you back into Ufton Fields Nature Reserve near the IBM hide at the Horseshoe Pool. The path along the western side of the reserve returns you to the car park.

Narrowboat cafe

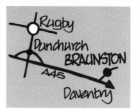

Start & finish The Millhouse public house near Braunston village on the A45 seven miles south of Rugby.
Parking The Millhouse car park (patrons only).
Terrain Canal towpaths and field paths. Possibility of mud after rain.
Time Allow three hours.
Facilities Pubs and shops at Braunston. Canalside pub and shop. Canalboat cafe. Pub at Willoughby.
Map Explorer sheet 222.

This walk contrasts the large village of Braunston and its busy canal and boatyard with the peaceful village of Willoughby and the open farmland between them.

1 From The Millhouse car park cross the bridge over the canal and go down to the towpath. Turn R and walk towards Braunston marina. Enjoy the picturesque canal boats and buildings and the village of Braunston on the hill across the canal. You can walk round the marina and rejoin the towpath further along.

Continue walking along the towpath passing the boat yards and the old engine house at bridge number two where there's also the first of the three locks on the walk.

At The Admiral Nelson pub cross a canal bridge and turn L along a lane back to Braunston village.

Where the lane turns sharp R go through the kissing gate straight ahead. Cross a field and join a footpath going R up a rising field to

The Admiral Nelson

the village. There are great views back to the canal from the hillside.

2 The path emerges into Braunston at the village green. Turn L to walk through the village passing many attractive and historic buildings. At the church turn R into Church Road and go through to a kissing gate at the crown of the bend signed 'Field Walk'.

Descend a hill and cross a canal bridge. Immediately turn L and go through a kissing gate into another field. Turn R and keep to the hedge on your R. Pass a pond in the second field and bear

30

slightly L to find a wide footbridge in the hedge ahead.

Keep straight on across the next two fields into a large triangular field. Head for the apex at the A45 road. Climb a stile and turn R to walk along the pavement to a petrol station and cafe – The Pantry – at edge of the village of Willoughby.

Take care crossing the A45 and turn L down the main street through the village. Pause at the Rose Inn for refreshment or just admire the thatched building, which looks just like a country pub should.

3 Pass the lonely-looking church at the western edge of the village and approx 50 yards beyond 30mph signs climb a stile in the hedge on your

L into a field. The long field, which shows signs of ancient ridge and furrow cultivation climbs gradually to a sparse hedge along the top. Bear R to a stile and cross two flat fields to Willoughby House.

At the country mansion, turn L through a farm gate to join a bridleway which keeps initially to the hedge on your L. Braunston is now a fine sight on a hill ahead. Descend gradually on the obvious route across four fields to the dismantled railway embankment which once carried the Rugby to Woodford Halse stretch of the Central Railway.

Go under the railway bridge, turn immediately R and go through a gate into a long field.

Keep to the hedge on your R and head for the church spire at Braunston. Go through a double gate and diagonally cross a field to a gate onto the A45.

Don't go onto the road. Instead, turn sharp R and descend some steps alongside the roadbridge to the canal towpath. Turn R and follow the curve of the canal around the small industrial area on your L.

Cross the beautiful double footbridge over the junction of the Grand Union and Oxford canals. Keep on the towpath, pass the Millhouse, and return to the roadbridge over the canal where the walk began.

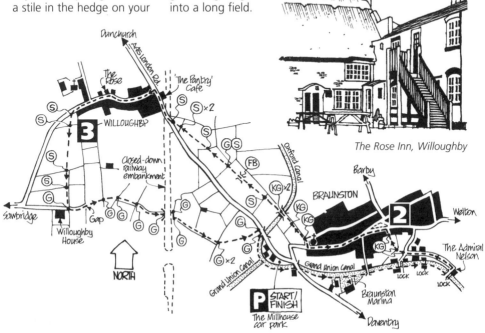

The Rose Inn, Willoughby

31

The Crown, Napton

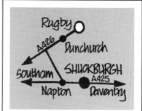

A glorious walk of rare delights. The deer park of a country estate, a unique and pretty village, colourful canal life and fantastic views from two of the highest hills in the district. Enjoy.

Start & Finish Lower Shuckburgh, eightr miles south of Rugby.
Parking Layby at the canal bridge in Lower Shuckburgh or with consideration on the minor road by the church.
Terrain Field paths, village streets and canal towpath. Some steep hills.
Time Allow three hours.
Facilities Pubs at Napton on the Hill.
Map Explorer sheet 222.

1 Begin walking up the lane towards the flamboyant Church of St John the Baptist, designed in 1864 by J Croft, 'a rogue architect'. The elaborately carved stonework of the building contrasts with the clipped churchyard yews and a six-sided tower supports an elegant spire.

Go over the main road (with care!) and find a stile into a field just to the L of the house opposite. Cross the field diagonally and climb the fields behind a group of red-brick houses. It's a steep climb but after a couple of fields you are rewarded with a great view back over Lower Shuckburgh – and a Millennium brazier!

Continue walking into the deer park. Nearby Shuckburgh Hall has been the home of the Shuckburgh family since the 11th century. The Hall is strictly private (please observe the signs in the park) but you can have a look at the little Church of St John the Baptist in the Wilderness, splendidly set overlooking Home Farm and the Northamptonshire countryside.

2 Turn R away from the church and follow the track which climbs alongside Long Side Wood to the highest point, Beacon Hill, the site of a deserted medieval village. The views are sensational.

Descend to the end of the wood, climb a stile and turn R. The village of Napton on the Hill is straight ahead, a fine sight, appropriately set on a hill a mile and a half away.

Go downhill, passing Halls Barn Farm on your L onto a narrow metalled

View over Lower Shuckburgh

32

House at Napton

road. Turn L along the road for a short distance then go through a gate R to initially follow a hedge on your R.

3 Head straight for Napton descending gradually through a series of gates and stiles to a minor road. Cross the road and climb a stile into a caravan site. Pass a fishing lake on your L, climb a stile into the next field and cross

diagonally to a minor road into Napton. Turn L along the road into the village.

Apart from its obvious aesthetic qualities, Napton is also unique, being the only example of a true hill settlement in the country. The hill on which it sits so grandly is twin-peaked; one occupied by the church, the other by a windmill.

Turn R up the village main street, passing the village green. Refreshment at the King's Head is highly recommended.

Continue walking up the footpath from the pub. Turn R at the top along a street of fine houses with fine views. Just before a road junction turn L into an enclosed pathway at the end of a terrace of houses.

4 Climb steeply to open ground near St Lawrence's Church, which dates back to the 13th century. The distant

windmill has been restored – with sails – as a private house and has records going back to 1542. The outlook from here is extensive and is said to include seven counties.

Keep straight on across the top of the hill and go down an enclosed pathway on the other side to the main road. Cross carefully and climb a stile to the R of a row of houses and diagonally cross a small field to a minor road. Turn L down the road towards Napton Marina. Cross the canal bridge and go down onto the towpath.

The remainder of the walk is along the canal towpath back to Lower Shuckburgh. It's full of interest – the marina, Napton Junction and, of course, the colourful narrow boats.

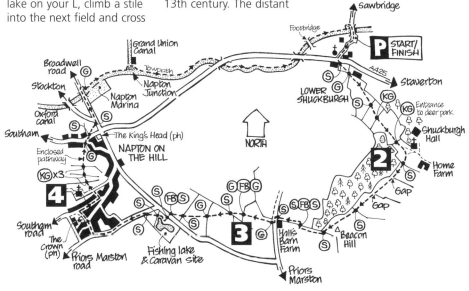

Church of St Giles, Chesterton

A wonderful walk across peaceful countryside featuring an ancient church and a series of beautiful, small lakes. Half the distance is on quiet estate roads through glorious open farmland.

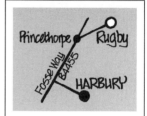

Start & finish Harbury, off the B4455 Fosse Way, 12 miles south of Rugby.
Parking The church and library car park, High Street or village hall, Park Lane.
Terrain Field paths and farm estate roads. Some gentle climbing.
Time Allow three hours.
Facilities Pubs and shops at Harbury.
Map Explorer sheet 206.

1 From the High Street car park walk up Chapel Street passing the Gamecock Inn. At the end of the street turn R into Park Lane which eventually brings you to the village Hall. Continue along Park Lane passing the New Old Inn.

At the end of the high wall of the last house in the village on your L find a signed stile into an enclosed footpath going downhill. Go through a gate and follow the hedge on your L on a marked route across five fields to a minor road. Cross the road and turn R along the grass verge for about 20 yards.

Pass a wide metal gate on your L and find a substantial wooden footbridge and stile into the adjoining field.

Harbury windmill

Cross two fields on the obvious route to a derelict red-brick building, Humble Bee Cottage. This was once the stable block and is, with the high wall in the next field, all that remains of the Peyto family manor house which was destroyed in 1902.

2 Go through a wide metal gate and immediately turn L to a narrow wooden gate into a meadow. With Chesterton church ahead descend to a footbridge and two stiles. Climb the next field to the church. Straight ahead is a beautiful red-brick gateway which was once the Peyto family entrance to the church. The gateway, to a design attributed to

Inigo Jones, dates back to around 1630 and was sensitively restored during 1988-90.

Turn L at the gateway and follow a sheep track to a wooden gate into the churchyard. The Church of St Giles was built in perpendicular style during Henry the Second's reign and has been altered and restored since. The Peyto family tomb dominates the east end.

The church is impressively set on a lonely hillock overlooking a tranquil duckpond. Go out of the churchyard and turn L along an unclassified minor road.

After about 500 yards walking beside a narrow pond go through a small wooden gate alongside a cattlegrid and entrance signed Kingston Farm. For much of the next three miles the route keeps to estate roads through beautiful and impressively well-kept farmland.

3 The road climbs gently around a hillside above a small lake edged by bullrushes and weeping willows to stately Kingston Manor Farm. Follow the road around the garden wall of the manor and descend to another lake populated by ducks, geese and heron. Continue through a small wood then climb again through an avenue of lime trees to Kingston Farm.

The road turns sharp L here then descends gently past a plantation of Christmas trees. Continue to a tee junction and turn L to Kingston Barn where there are a number of large barns and a couple of houses. You may also come across pheasants here. The final stretch of estate road is part of the Centenary Way and exits the farm estate at the Warwick to Bishop Itchington road.

4 Cross the road and take the middle one of the three roads at the junction which is signed Bush Heath Lane. As you approach the village sign for Harbury, find a metal gate in the hedge on your R and cross a field to a copse of trees. Another gate gives access to a long playing field. Walk along the long field back to the village hall.

Harbury is a large village with many fine houses and a dramatic windmill conversion towering above High Street. Nearby Chesterton Windmill is worth visiting both for the architecture and the extensive views.

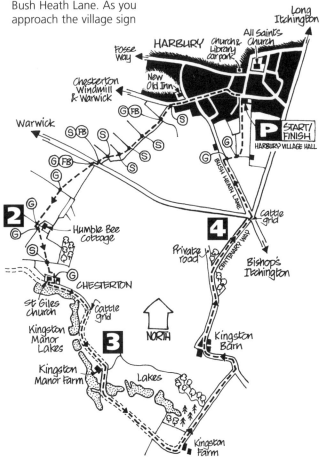

35

Hatton Workshops

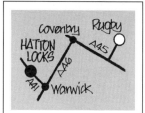

Start & finish Hatton Locks, on the Grand Union Canal 17 miles west of Rugby.
Parking Pay & display car park at Hatton Workshops.
Terrain Canal towpath, lanes and field paths. Expect mud.
Time Allow three hours.
Facilities Cafe and restaurant at the car park. The Waterman pub nearby.
Map Explorer sheet 221.

An interesting walk contrasting a mile and a half stretch of fourteen locks on the Grand Union Canal and farmland to the north of Hatton village.

1 Go down onto the canal towpath and begin walking south east towards Warwick. The going is easy and the towpath and locks well-maintained. The tower of St Mary's Church, Warwick is prominent on the skyline ahead.

Warwick and Birmingham Canal was started in 1793 and amalgamated with other companies in 1929 to form what is now known as the Grand Union Canal. The 22 mile-long canal was finally opened in 1800. With the increase in traffic to coal merchants and warehouses in Warwick the canal was widened to its present width in 1934. There are a total of 21 locks at Hatton, 17 between Hatton

Workshops and the A46 road bridge and another 4 north west of the former.

The towpath passes under two concrete bridges, one sadly – but appropriately – called 'Ugly Bridge'.

The route leaves the towpath at the third bridge (No.51) but it's well worth walking the extra 200 yards

Wedgnock Park farmhouse

of so on the towpath for a look at the delightful cottage beside the last lock before the A46 road bridge (lock No.27).

Return to bridge No.27 and find a narrow footpath which climbs to Coach House Cottage and Old Budbrooke Road. Cross the road and head up the hill to cross the A4177 at traffic lights.

2 Join a metalled road straight ahead which goes round the edge of a field to Wedgnock Park Farm. The aspect is now open and pleasantly rural.

Go through a metal gate beside the farmhouse and turn sharp L as requested by the waymarking signs

36

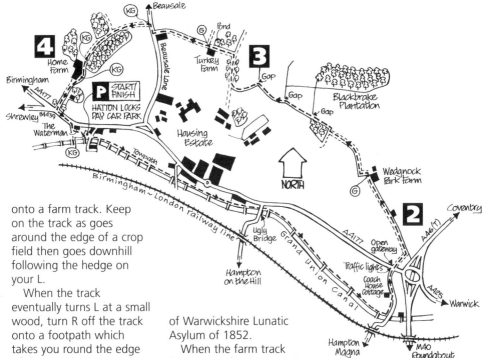

onto a farm track. Keep on the track as goes around the edge of a crop field then goes downhill following the hedge on your L.

When the track eventually turns L at a small wood, turn R off the track onto a footpath which takes you round the edge of the wood. Keep on the obvious path close to the hedge on your L. A modern housing estate can now be seen on your L.

3 At a bridleway, which goes into the housing estate, turn R along the bridleway as it rises up a hill between an avenue of trees. To your R there's a terrific view of Warwick and beyond.

At the top of the hill turn L onto another bridleway which takes you past Turkey Farm onto a farm track. The former Central and King Edward VII hospitals, closed in 1995 and now incorporated into a modern housing estate are prominent on a hill to your L. They include the Jacobean-style County

of Warwickshire Lunatic Asylum of 1852.

When the farm track joins Beausale Lane turn R along the lane for a short distance then go L through a metal kissing gate onto a rough track which crosses an open field towards a wood.

4 Keep on the track as it swings R to a gap in the wood and heads towards Home Farm. Just before the farmyard, turn L off the track onto an enclosed footpath which takes you around the farm buildings.

Join the metalled road leading away from the farm to the main A4177 road. Cross the road – with care! – to The Waterman car park and possible

refreshment at the inn.

There's also a terrific view of the canal and locks from the rear of the inn to enjoy. Go down the grassy hill through The Waterman's garden to return to the car park where the walk began.

Bottom Lock Cottage

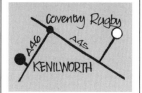

The castle ruins from the lane to High House Farm

Start & finish Kenilworth Castle, 14 miles west of Rugby.
Parking Castle pay car park or free car park at Castle Green.
Terrain Lanes, tracks and wide grass verge of main road. Expect mud.
Time Allow three hours.
Facilities The Claverdon Arms near the castle.
Map Explorer sheet 221.

A wonderful circuit across estate land and through woodland with the red-sandstone ruins of Kenilworth Castle the romantic star of the show.

1 From the pay car park begin walking along the main avenue – 'The Causeway', once used for jousting in the Middle Ages – to the castle. Swing R at the castle wall to follow the footpath around the wall to the free car park at the Earl of Leicester's Gatehouse on Castle Green.

Descend to a narrow footpath between the high north wall and the grassy bank of Castle Green. Emerge into an open, grassy area around the castle. Keep straight on, passing a thatched house on your R to find a gate into a lane.

Turn L up the lane which rises gradually to High House Farm. The view opens up and the full panorama of the castle is revealed behind you. The area to your L was once the Royal hunting park and site of 'The Great Mere' which almost surrounded the castle with water.

Enter an enclosed footpath to the R of High House Farm which takes you to the site of Henry V's 'Pleasaunce' – or pleasure

A door in the castle walls

house – where the King could relax with ... er ... 'royal pleasures'.

Ignore the lane going L, instead walk straight across the field heading between the raised 'pleasure' area and a impressive plantation of what looks like pampas grass.

2 Keep straight on and go through a metal kissing gate to follow a hedge first on your L and then on your R. The way ahead is obvious, along a broad track between low, tree-covered hills. You are now crossing Honiley Farm Estate with game birds your likely companions. The spire of St John Baptist Church at Honiley pokes above the trees to your L ahead.

When you reach a footbridge, cross it to rising ground beyond and immediately turn R to follow a stream as it meanders up the RHS of a crop field. Keep straight on, climbing up the R of the next field and, following the waymarkers, swing R then L into a large, level field. A track across it brings you to the A4177 Honiley Road.

Turn R to walk along the wide grass verge of the busy road. Pass the entrance to Holly Farm Business Park and a roadsign which may be a surprise as it says, 'Welcome to Solihull'. (Didn't seem that far to walk!)

3 Keep on the grass verge as the road swings R then enter a enclosed pathway on your R, waymarked 'Bridleway'. Pass behind some houses and continue on a track through Poors Wood where

Cottages at Castle Green

there's a spectacular display of bluebells in springtime.

Exit the wood and follow the hedge on your R down a hill to Warriors Lodge Farm. Follow the signs through the farmyard onto a concrete road.

Join Chase Lane on the edge of Chase Wood – another venue for spectacular displays of bluebells. Signs on the trees (and possible shooting parties) make clear that the wood is 'Strictly Private'.

There now follows about a mile of pleasant level walking along Chase Lane.

4 At three red-brick houses on your L go

through a metal kissing gate opposite – signed 'Kenilworth Castle 1 mile'. As you cross the four fields back to the castle grounds the view of the ruins ahead is sensational.

To return to the castle pay car park walk south around the walls back to The Causeway.

Two buildings dominate the ruins: the massive 12th-century Keep and the great Hall built by John of Gaunt in the 14th century. The castle, which was visited three times by Elizabeth the First, was destroyed by Cromwell's men during the English Civil War.

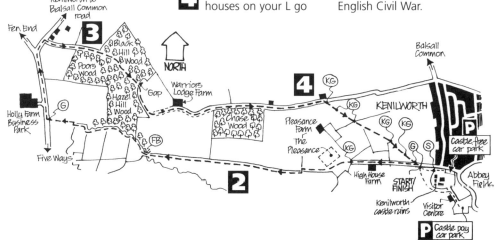

St Mary's Church and the lane out of Everdon

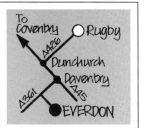

A superb walk across the rolling Northamptonshire countryside. Visit two picturesque villages and stately Fawsley Park. Hilly, with extensive views throughout.

1 Leave Everdon down the lane between the The Plough and St Mary's Church. After a short distance turn L off the lane to walk through some allotments signed 'Spencer Charity'. Cross diagonally over the field below the allotments and climb a stile near the bottom L corner of the hedge. Cross three pastures to join the hard surfaced road to Snorscomb Farm. Go through the farm gate on your R and keep on the drive which follows the hedge on your R around the farm buildings.

Where the lane swings R go through a gate on your L onto a signed bridleway which rises steeply across three fields to a minor road between Preston Capes and Upper Stow. Admire the view back over Everdon then turn R along the broad grass verge of the minor road to join the northern end of the Knightly Way.

2 Preston Capes is on a hill ahead as the road descends steeply to pass through a level crop field. Before reaching the farm buildings on your L turn R off the road and cross to a waymarked stile in a hedge and climb a steep pasture to the recently renovated Manor Farm on the edge of Preston Capes.

The village was part of the Fawsley estate

Cottage doorway, Preston Capes

Start & finish Everdon, 12 miles south of Rugby.
Parking Roadside with consideration. Best across road from the Field Centre.
Terrain Field paths, bridleways and quiet minor roads across crop fields. Some steep hills. Expect mud after rain.
Time Allow three hours.
Facilities The Plough at Everdon.
Map Explorer sheet 206.

until 1932, when the last surviving family member, Sir Charles Knightley, died and the property, including the villages of Charwelton and Badby, was divided into lots and sold at auction.

Preston Capes is too pretty to leave without a look round so turn L up the hill to the road junction then return and go along Old Forge Lane past the village hall. The Church of St Peter and St Paul is over 500 years old and some graves in the churchyard date back to the 1600s.

Leave the village down the road at the north end. Go over a stile in the hedge on your L waymarked 'Knightley

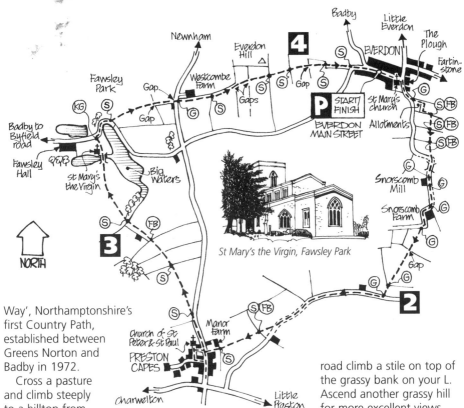

St Mary's the Virgin, Fawsley Park

Way', Northamptonshire's first Country Path, established between Greens Norton and Badby in 1972.

Cross a pasture and climb steeply to a hilltop from where there's excellent views of Preston Capes and Fawsley Park. Descend across two well-waymarked fields to a stile into the park.

3 The main park is now hidden by a grassy hill and it is a rare treat as the classic landscape of Fawsley Hall, the lonely little church on a hill and the lake is gradually revealed as you walk over the hilltop.

Fawsley Hall and the landscaped park was created by the Knightley family. After they bought the manor of Fawsley in 1416 the family lived here for over 500 years.

The hall was requisitioned during the first and second world wars but began to deteriorate in the 1960s. A new owner, Mr E.A. Saunders, began renovation in 1975 and eventually the hall was reopened in its present reincarnation as a luxury hotel. St Mary's the Virgin Church dates back to the 13th century and contains the Knightley family tombs.

Keep on the track past the church and go through a gate onto the minor road through the park. Turn R along the road around the northern end of the Big Waters. Just before you come to a cattle grid in the road climb a stile on top of the grassy bank on your L. Ascend another grassy hill for more excellent views back to Fawsley Park.

4 The route continues in a more or less straight line back to Everdon but there's also another climb up to the top of Everdon Hill and yet more extensive views. The final descent into Everdon is steep and the village is not seen until the last moment.

St Mary's Church, Everdon dates from the 14th century with evidence of an older building on the site. It has been claimed that the churchyard, and not the one at Stoke Poges, was the inspiration for Grey's famous elegy 'In a English Churchyard'.

Honey Hill Farm & Honey Hill

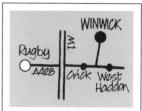

Start & finish Winwick, nine miles east of Rugby.
Parking Difficult, but with consideration on side of narrow village roads. There are wide grass verges. Best bet up road signed 'No Through Road' where walk starts. Please do not park in roadside laybys obviously provided for residents.
Terrain Bridleways, field paths and canal towpath. Some hills. Expect mud.
Time Allow three hours.
Facilities None.
Map Explorer sheet 223.

A hidden-away picturesque hamlet, country mansions, a superb hilltop viewpoint, an imaginative golf course and a peaceful stretch of the Grand Union Canal – this a route to savour.

1 Begin walking up the lane signed 'No Through Road' at Bridge Cottage to the classic Victorian, Winwick Hall, built in 1850 at a cost of £2,000. The distinctive 'Crinkle-Crackle Wall' at the hall gates was built, using 60,000 hand-made bricks, to celebrate the Millennium. The walls, designed for their strength in windy areas, were popular in Victorian times. The gates, riveted not welded, weigh over 2 tonnes each.

Continue up a hard-surfaced track opposite the hall, signed 'Jurassic Way'. Pass the entrance to Home Farm and climb over a hill. Where the track swings L to Winwick Lodge, keep straight ahead through a gate into an enclosed grassy track signed 'Byway'. Climb up the hill with a hedge on your L. Where the hedge ends, turn L across the slope of the field on a path signed 'Bridleway to Honey Hill'. Descend slightly and go through a wide metal gate. Turn R to follow the hedge on your R and continue into a large crop field.

Cold Ashby Golf Club

Bridge cottage

is on the hill on your R. The 27 hole course, 'set in rolling terrain' is used for skiing when snow stops the golf.

2 Continue to the end of the large field and turn L for a short distance to find steps down a steep bank to part of the golf course. Cross a fairway and ascend steps to cross another narrow section of the course. Go through a gate and cross a field to Honey Hill Farm. The going begins to steepen now and an extensive view is opening out behind you. Go onto the hard-surfaced farm road and climb above the farm buildings. Pause to appreciate the fantastic view back to Rugby, Daventry and beyond.

The box warehouses at Crick are an appalling blot on the landscape and an example of how commerce is allowed to make a mess of the countryside with little apparent control. Why can't they be painted green instead of white?

Continue over the brow of the hill and turn L along the minor Swinford to Cold Ashby road where a new view across the A12 towards Lutterworth is revealed.

St Michael & All Angels, Winwick

After a short distance where the road swings R, turn L onto an enclosed track signed 'Jurrasic Way. Bridleway'. The route descends gradually along the side of Honey Hill where a stone memorial commemorates the opening of the 88-mile Jurrasic Way from Banbury to Stamford.

As you pass a small wood on your L, bear R to some gorse bushes where a path descends steeply to a wide metal gate out of the field into an enclosed pathway which takes you to the hamlet of Elkington.

3 You can now turn L along a byway back to Winwick. Or, if you're like me and like to see narrowboats chugging through the countryside, turn R along the road to a bridge and access to the Grand Union Canal.

The next two miles are a pleasant walk along a wide and grassy towpath which meanders through woodland and open countryside.

4 At the fifth canal bridge leave the towpath and join a hard-surfaced lane to Winwick Grange. Just past the farmhouse, turn L and climb a stile into an open field signed 'Footpath to Winwick'. Keep straight on across the field to another stile and a footbridge.

In the next field bear L heading for the tower of Winwick Church. Join an enclosed pathway and, passing the impressive Manor House, re-enter Winwick near St Michael's and All Angels Church.

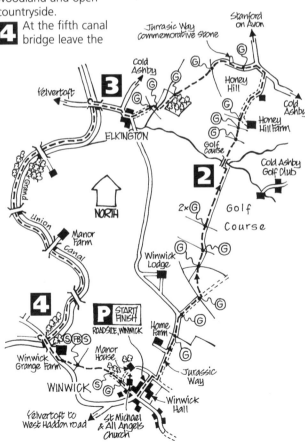